Awakened Mind

The Master Class Series

Awakened Mind

How Thoughts Create Reality

A MASTER CLASS COURSE WITH

Mitch Horowitz

MEDIA

Published 2019 by Gildan Media LLC
aka G&D Media
www.GandDmedia.com

FIRST EDITION 2019

Front Cover design by David Rheinhardt of Pyrographx

Interior design by Meghan Day Healey of Story Horse, LLC

Library of Congress Cataloging-in-Publication Data is available upon request

ISBN: 978-1-7225-0188-4

10   9   8   7   6   5   4   3   2   1

Contents

Introduction

Welcome to the Master Class series. Each of these courses instructs you, in ten simple, straightforward lessons, how to benefit from the causative powers of your mind.

The lessons are designed so that you may experience one each day, or all of them at once. Do the exercises in your own time and at your own pace—but is crucial that you do them. At the end of each course you'll find a short quiz to reinforce your knowledge.

The Master Class series provides you with new and practical ways of excelling at life. Feel free to email me personally with any questions at: MasterClassWithMitch@gmail.com.

Lesson
ONE

Your Mental Frontiers

This course teaches you how to use your mind to transform your life. We are not going to explore "cutting edge" cognitive studies or neuroscience breakthroughs. No. If you want that, click onto a Ted Talk or any of the pop-science brain trends written about online.

Rather, we are aiming for a total revolution in your existence, a new sense of who you are, and of the unseen faculties and agencies that you possess. This course is a hands-on application of a misunderstood field: **positive-mind metaphysics.**

You've probably heard critics running down "positive thinking" as a namby-pamby philosophy of wishful thoughts and popular delusion. I have studied the field for ten years, and documented it as a historian and personal seeker. I promise you this: the critics are wrong. The seemingly familiar terrain of positive thinking can unlock a new world of self-potential for you.

Do you doubt that? Use this course's ten simple lessons—or any one of them—to put my claim to the test. If what I write here doesn't work for you, discard my claims. But if it does work, not only will you only gain a significant new measure of self-respect, creativity, and vibrancy, but you will question everything that you have been taught about what it means to be human.

The foundational principle of this course is the one simple idea that *thoughts are causative.* How do I mean that? Do we live under an overarching mental super law, sometimes called the Law of Attraction? No. We live under many laws and forces. But thought is one exquisitely effective, and little understood, aspect of life. Our thoughts co-create our lives in ways that we have not yet understood.

A bit of history before we get our hands dirty. Positive-mind metaphysics is rooted in a wave of therapeutic spiritual experiments in mid-to-late 19th century New England, which followed from the writings of Ralph Waldo Emerson. Freethinkers probed how our thoughts impact reality. I call their approach "applied Transcendentalism." It became popularly known as the "power of positive thinking—or New Thought.

Before we go further, I have a vital piece of advice. One factor, more than any other, will determine how you experience this course: your depth of hunger for self-change. As an Arab proverb goes: "The way bread tastes depends on how hungry you are." The key to every self-help program is to *approach it as if your life depends on it.* If you do that, you will discover extraordinary new possibilities.

Lesson
TWO

The Three-Step Miracle

Here is a way to start thinking differently about how you use your mind. Imagine that a genie offered you a wish, but with a catch: You had to tell him the truth about what you *really* wanted—otherwise you'd lose everything.

We repeatedly tell ourselves what we think we want ("a better house," "a new love," etc.), but rarely subject our desires and wishes to mature, sustained scrutiny. Often, *we do not know what we want from life at all.*

A powerful, simple exercise will blow open how you think about your desires. I call it the Three-Step Miracle. The exercise comes from a beguiling little pamphlet published anonymously in 1926 under the title *It Works.* In actuality, the author was a Chicago salesman named Roy Herbert Jarrett (1874–1937). Jarrett tested his theory for years and didn't put it in writing until he was past the age of 50.

This program consists of three simple steps. Remember: To benefit you must do them with total commitment.

1. **Carefully devise a list of what you *really* want from life.** Revise it, rewrite it, and work on it every day. Throw your certainties out the window. Keep rewriting and reorganizing your list until it feels absolutely right.

2. **Read your list morning, noon, and night; think about it always.** Commit to reading it in a quiet, contemplative atmosphere each morning upon waking; again at midday; and once more just before drifting to sleep at night. (Later you'll see why this timing is important.) Carry it with you in a pocket notebook or on a laminated index card.

3. **Tell no one what you are doing.** You must keep your list to yourself. This is not to cultivate some air of mystery but rather to prevent others—friends, relatives, coworkers—from making casually negative comments that shake your resolve (a favorite human pas-

time). These dreams belong to *you*. They are intimate, powerful, and private.

Then, express gratitude each time results arrive.

That's it? Yes, that's it. How can something so simple really work? Because this exercise pushes us to do something that we think we do all time but rarely try: *Honestly come to terms with our innermost desires.* Most of us drift through life lazily thinking that we want a new house, a loving mate, a better job, and so on. But the things that we repeat inside can merely mirror what we believe would make us look good in the eyes of others, or what our upbringing or our peers tell us we should want. Or our desires may be fleeting fantasies—we want ice cream, so to speak, until the next thing catches our eye. All of this can obfuscate our most authentic aims and yearnings.

Ask yourself once more: Have you ever sat down, in a mature and sustained manner, stripped of all convention and inhibition, and probed, with unsparing honesty, what you really want from life? Someone who scoffs at money may discover that he truly craves wealth. A person who has dedicated herself to promoting others may find that she hungers for the spotlight. A corporate climber may see that he just wants a quiet life at home.

You cannot harness the mental assets covered in this course unless you know where you want to go. When you do, you will discover resources that you never knew you had.

Lesson
THREE

Wealth and Health

Some books promulgate the notion that positive-mind techniques can produce everything from money to health to love from out of the ether. I feel strongly that no reader or seeker should ever be handed an over-promise—or should rely on a single method. Use all the resources around you: medical, physical, financial, moral—and mental.

I mentioned earlier that I do not believe we live under one mental super-law, sometimes called the Law of Attraction. We live under many laws and forces, of which the creative potentials of the mind are one important part. I want to make it clear that the mind alone is not a magic wand. It surely *does* have a role in health and wealth—but not always in the ways that we believe.

I recently discovered a cache of letters that readers had sent to writer Joseph Murphy (1898-1981) more than a decade after the New Thought pioneer's death. It was heartbreaking to read the yearning questions of these earnest correspondents, many of whom wondered why Murphy's techniques weren't working for them. I selected one letter below, handwritten by a woman in Tampa, Florida, that typified the needs of many who wrote him. If I could reach back in time and respond to this woman, here is what I would say:

August 12, 1993

Dear Dr. Murphy,

I keep reading your book Your Infinite Power to Be Rich *so much that it is falling apart and I still haven't reached my goal of receiving abundance.*

I feel that I must be doing something wrong so that I can't break this poverty syndrome. I keep saying these wonderful affirmations but I think I neutralize them because I don't believe I deserve wealth of any kind.

I would like to be financially secure so that I never have to worry about money again. I would like good, supportive relationships and a soul mate.

Somehow I got the impression from my youth that I didn't deserve anything because

I'm no good.

Please help me to get out of my poverty.

Sincerely, _____

Dear _____,

*First of all I want to assure you of something—
and I want you to remember this for the rest
of your life: You are not only good—*you are
exceptional. *You are a leader among people
and are part of the nobles of the human race.
This is for the simple fact that you have taken
steps that so few people ever consider: striving to heighten your place in life, engaging in
inner development, and caring enough about
such things to take the time to write a letter to
an author whose work touched you. Most people never write one letter in their lives. Most
never read a single book, or attend a single
lecture, with the aim of raising their sense of
self-potential. So, please, let us lay that childhood myth immediately to rest. You are exceptional—and this is a fact.*

*I love Joseph Murphy's work; but I believe
that sometimes saying an affirmation—even
with depth of feeling—is not enough. The most
remarkable people in history, from Joan of
Arc to Mahatma Gandhi, led lives of faith*
and *action. They were ardently committed to*

affecting things in the world. Whatever your employment, throw yourself into it with passion. Be aware of everything that you can do for your bosses, coworkers, and customers. Be the problem-solver to whom others look for help and advisement. Know more about your job than everyone else, not in a know-it-all way but with the aim of providing service and doing your personal best. Expect—and respectfully require—good wages for your good work. Join a union if you are able, and support activists and leaders who defend the rights of workers. But, above all, be the person upon whom all others rely.

Author James Allen was a working-class Englishman who rose from a childhood of poverty to a writing career, largely through his dignity of character and his dogged and intelligent persistence. I urge you to read his As a Man Thinketh. *And when you do, remember that his words and ideas weren't the work of someone famous or wealthy. They came from a working person who had tested them in the laboratory of his own life. Also please read Napoleon Hill's* Think and Grow Rich, *which is useful because it combines a program of mental metaphysics with a plan of action.*

As for good relationships and finding a soul mate, those, too, are noble and right yearnings. My council is to associate only with people who are supportive and respectful of your search for self-betterment and spiritual awareness. Seek out those who are engaged, in whatever way, in bettering themselves. Spend no time—or as little time as practicality allows—among cynics, bullies, or unproductive people. Avoid those who gossip, and refuse to listen to rumors or hearsay. Do this, and you will naturally come into the company of true friends and, hopefully, a soul mate.

I enter into a few moments of prayer every day at 3 p.m. EST—and I would be privileged if you would join me. I wish you every good thing.

Your friend, Mitch

Lesson
FOUR

The Mind and Money

Because I've noted the limits of the mind's positive powers that does not mean that the mind cannot help us win the game of the life. It can. In his *Think and Grow Rich* (1937), the motivational writer Napoleon Hill (1883–1970) provided what I consider the finest modern program of self-development.

Hill's techniques can be used in pursuit of any valid aim, not just money. *Think and Grow Rich* should be on the bookshelf of every artist, teacher, intellectual, soldier, and activist—anyone with a passionate sense of purpose in life. Here is a digest of Hill's program:

1. **Definite Chief Aim.** Without an absolutely rock-solid sense of the *one thing* you wish to accomplish above all else, nothing is possi-

ble. Write down your aim. This is no trifle—this is your life.

2. **Master Mind Group.** You must form a group of likeminded strivers—as small as two or as large as six or seven—with whom you feel entirely at ease, trustful, and harmonious. (This is not easy—choose carefully.) Meet either in person or digitally at regular intervals to discuss each member's plans and ideas, and to share encouragement and counsel. This will multiply the intellect, drive, and inventiveness of each member. It is easy to neglect this step. Do not.

3. **Enthusiasm.** This is the force on which all accomplishment depends. *You must love something in order to attain it.* You must select an aim that instills in you boundless enthusiasm and passion. With those emotive forces at work, you will gain remarkable resilience and power.

4. **Golden Rule.** This is the simplest and yet subtlest ethical code in human history. Study it. Consider it. Let it inform each step of your life—including *your thoughts* and *your choice of an aim.*

5. **Action.** Hill's program is not one of "wishing." You must devise concrete, reasonable plans to carry out your Definite Chief Aim. Educate yourself. Be bold but realistic in your plans. And act on them. *Begin!*

6. **Accurate Thinking.** There are two types of information: the useful and the useless. The useful is anything that advances your aim. The useless is rumor, opinion, gossip, hostile criticism, and sarcasm. Restrict your thoughts, conversations, and information intake to the first kind.

7. **Failure.** Success often arrives after many temporary setbacks. This is a rule. When faced with failure, conceive of it as a temporary setback. *Plan anew.*

Here is *Think and Grow Rich* in a nutshell: **Emotionalized thought directed toward one passionately held aim—aided by organized planning and the Master Mind—is the root of all accomplishment.**

Lesson
FIVE

The Thirty-Day
Mental Challenge

American philosopher William James (1842–
1910) yearned to find a practical philosophy,
one that produced concrete improvements in
happiness.

The Harvard physician grew encouraged,
especially in his final years, by his personal experiments with New Thought, which he called
"the religion of healthy-mindedness." I challenge people today to continue James's search
for a testable, workable system of ethical and
spiritual development. Try this thirty-day experiment that puts positive-mind dynamics to
the test.

The exercise is based on a passage from a
1931 book, *Body, Mind, and Spirit* by Elwood
Worcester and Samuel McComb, in which a

prominent scientist describes radically improving his life through a one-month thought experiment. I have condensed his testimony:

Up to my fiftieth year I was unhappy, ineffective, and obscure. I had read some New Thought literature and some statements of William James on directing one's attention to what is good and useful and ignoring the rest. Such ideas seemed like bunk—but feeling that life was intolerable I determined to subject them to a month-long test.

During this time I resolved to impose definite restrictions on my thoughts. In thinking of the past, I would dwell only on its pleasing incidents. In thinking of the present, I would direct attention to its desirable elements. In thinking of the future, I would regard every worthy and possible ambition as within reach.

I threw myself into this experiment. I was soon surprised to feel happy and contented. But the outward changes astonished me more. I deeply craved the recognition of certain eminent men. The foremost of these wrote me, out of the blue, inviting me to become his assistant. All my books were published. My colleagues grew helpful and cooperative.

It seems that I stumbled upon a path of life, *and set forces working for me which were previously working against me.*

Here is how devise your own experiment: 1) Choose your start date. 2) Write out the entire testimony above by hand. This helps you remember it and feel a sense of ownership over it. 3) After you have written it, create a personal contract by adding: "I dedicate myself on this day of ＿＿＿＿＿ to focus on all that is nourishing, advancing, and promising for thirty days (signed) ＿＿＿＿＿＿＿＿＿."

Feel free to email me your results (or questions) at MasterClassWithMitch@gmail.com. I will personally read and reply to each email.

Lesson
SIX

Stronger Every Day

We hear a lot today about using "affirmations"—repeat phrases that are supposed to help bolster our confidence and focus us on our goals. I believe that affirmations can be effective, so long as they do not chaff against overwhelmingly contrary feelings or facts. Then we get into a mental battle with ourselves.

A French hypnotherapist, Emile Coué (1857–1926) devised one of the earliest—and still the best—affirmative-mind programs. Although Coué's name may be unfamiliar, you have probably heard of his confidence-boosting mantra: "Day by day, in every way, I am getting better and better."

Coué won thousands of followers in the early 1920s, but critics mocked his formula for its singsong simplicity and today he is forgotten. The mind pioneer deserves a new look, however. Placebo researchers at Harvard Medical School recently validated one of Coué's core insights.

In January 2014, a medical school study reported that migraine sufferers responded better to medication when given "positive information" about a drug. Coué made that exact observation in the early 1900s while working as a pharmacist in northwestern France. He found that patients benefited more from their medication when he spoke in praise of a formula—which led to his famous mantra.

Coué believed that anyone, with almost any need, could stimulate the same positive mental forces he saw among patients by gently whispering the "day by day" affirmation twenty times before drifting to sleep at night and again on waking. He called it "conscious autosuggestion." In 1922, Coué described his program this way:

> *Every morning on awakening and every evening as soon as you are in bed, close your eyes, and without fixing your attention on what you say, pronounce twenty times, just loud enough so that you may hear your own words, the following phrase, using a string with twenty knots in it for counting: 'DAY BY DAY, IN EVERY WAY, I AM GETTING BETTER AND BETTER.' The words: 'IN EVERY WAY'*

being good for anything and everything, it is not necessary to formulate particular auto-suggestions. Make this autosuggestion with faith and confidence, and with the certainty that you are going to obtain what you desire.

It is very important to follow Coué's directions about using the formula just before drifting off at night and just upon waking in the morning. Scientists sometimes call the period when you hover between sleep and consciousness the hypnagogic state. At such times your mind is uniquely impressionable. During the hypnagogic state your conscious and subconscious minds are fused, so to speak, which is why you may notice hallucinatory experiences. Also, emotions, such as such as grief or worry, can take on greater intensity. It is a very sensitive period. But you can *use* this time for positive ends by employing the day-by-day formula.

More than a century later, the Harvard Medical School paper, while echoing Coué's original insight, made no mention of the mind theorist. But Coue's work is known to one of the study's architects, Ted Kaptchuk, who directs Harvard's program in placebo research. "Of course I know about Coué," Kaptchuk told me, agreeing that the migraine study could coalesce with Coué's observations.

Try "Day by day"—you may be surprised.

Lesson
SEVEN

The Inner Golden Rule

I want to open today's lesson with a confession. Shortly before I began writing these words, I felt that some unnamed factor was stymying my progress in life. Something was limiting my ability to envision and pursue higher possibilities for myself and others. I was stuck in a holding pattern.

The key to my problem appeared in the Golden Rule. The precept "do unto others as you would have them do unto you" runs through virtually every religious and ethical teaching, from the Talmud to the Gospels to the Bhagavad Gita. Dubbed the Golden Rule in late-seventeenth century England, this dictum can today seem overly familiar or clichéd. But the Golden Rule holds an inner truth that can make all the difference in your life.

In his 1928 book *The Law of Success*, Napoleon Hill related the Golden Rule to the phenomenon of autosuggestion, or the suggestions we continually make to ourselves. What we internally repeat and believe takes root in our subconscious and shapes our self-image and perceptions of the surrounding world. This is a profound and determinative fact.

But note carefully: the same autosuggestive process is also triggered by *what we think about others*. "Your thoughts of others are registered in your subconscious mind through the principle of autosuggestion," Hill wrote, "thereby building your own character in exact duplicate." Hence: "You must 'think of others as you wish them to think of you.'"

Let's consider Hill's point of view more fully:

> *Stated in another way, every act and every thought you release modifies your own character in exact conformity with the nature of the act or thought, and your character is a sort of center of magnetic attraction, which attracts to you the people and conditions that harmonize with it. You cannot indulge in an act toward another person without having first created the nature of that act in your own*

thought, and you cannot release a thought without planting the sum and substance and nature of it in your own subconscious mind, there to become a part and parcel of your own character.

Grasp this simple principle and you will understand why you cannot afford to hate or envy another person. You will also understand why you cannot afford to strike back, in kind, at those who do you an injustice. Likewise, you will understand the injunction, "Return good for evil."

When we indulge in fantasies of revenge or score settling—which I've done during morning shaves more times than I can count—we not only shackle ourselves to past wrongs, but also to the wrongs that we would do in exchange. Our acts of violence, whether by mind, talk, or hand, reenact themselves in our psyches and perceptions. We are lowered to the level of people we resent or even hate when we counter—mentally or otherwise—their type of behavior. An adjunct to the Golden Rule is: We become what we don't forgive.

Conversely, thoughts of generosity and forgiveness add a special solidity to our character, Hill notes, "that gives it life and power."

Our thoughts about ourselves and about others can be seen as an invisible engine that molds our character and experience. This is why it is extremely important to abstain from spreading or listening to gossip or character as- sassination.

If you find yourself bumping against limits, or having difficulty formulating and acting on your plans, reconsider your relationship to the Golden Rule.

Lesson
EIGHT

Daily Bread

I want to supply you with a list of daily practices that I personally use. If done with commitment and consistency, these simple techniques will produce changes in your inner and outer experience. Everything here fits within the parameters of a busy day.

1. **Morning Connection.** Upon waking it is crucial to make some connection to your highest ideals—do this *before* picking up your iPhone, clicking on the television, or getting sucked into social media. You can practice something very basic, such as saying The Lord's Prayer or, if you prefer something non-spiritual, repeating an affirmation while still in bed, such as Emile Coué's "Day by day."

2. **Sacred Literature.** Connect each day, however briefly, with a great piece of ethical or religious literature. Even if it's just one line from the Book of Proverbs, carry it in your mind throughout the day. I am registered to receive a daily email with a passage from mystical teacher Vernon Howard (anewlife .org). You can also carry a pocket Bible, Bhagavad Gita, or Tao Te Ching, or keep one on your phone. Read it in the elevator, on your commute, or at your desk.

3. **Express Gratitude.** As Joni Mitchell sang, "Don't it always seem to go that you don't know what you've got till it's gone." These words are prophecy. We bypass incredible blessings each day. After actor Christopher Reeve was rendered quadriplegic in an accident he observed: "I see somebody just get up out of a chair and stretch and I go, 'No, you're not even thinking about what you're doing and how lucky you are to do that.'" Every morning—no matter what stresses you face—enumerate at least three things for which you are grateful. It will set your day on a different track.

4. **Three P.M. Prayer.** In Christian tradition, Jesus is said to have died on the cross at 3 p.m. Some people reserve this as a spe-

cial time for prayer—even if just to take a few moments to express thanks, remember a loved one, or ask to be of highest service that day. I set a daily alarm on my phone for 3 p.m. and often use this time to pray for someone's recovery, or for the needs of friends or people who have written to me. However packed your schedule, you can almost always find a few moments for a silent devotion. I invite everyone reading this to join me—whether once in a while or every day—at 3 p.m. EST for a few moments of meditation or silent prayer.

5. **Choose Kindness.** Toward the end of his life, the twentieth-century novelist and spiritual journeyer Aldous Huxley was asked by a reporter to name—out of all the Eastern philosophies, psychedelic experiments, and human potential exercises the British intellectual had tried—the single best method for inner development. "Just try being a little kinder," Huxley replied. The seeker wasn't being glib. Christ, Buddha, and the Talmudic sages recognized kindness as a revolutionary act.

6. **Radically Forgive.** Nelson Mandela did not bring justice to South Africa so much as forgiveness and reconciliation. The thirst for

justice often translates into spite and vengeance, which is life withering on both a national and intimate scale. Commit daily to an authentic effort to forgive everyone who has hurt you, even cruel people. If you can honestly attempt this—and it may require a lifetime of repeat tries—you will begin to exprerience a new sense of inner calm. Remember: *We become what we don't forgive.*

7. **Say No to Humiliation.** Much of our social media, talk radio, and "reality" television dishes out the cruel glee of seeing someone get embarrassed or humiliated. During the day, whether on your phone, computer, or in front of the television, avoid posts and shows that drag people through the mud. Are you tempted to make a snarky remark on Twitter? Ask yourself: *Is this necessary?* The ancient Greeks cautioned to respect your neighbor's privacy and dignity: "Zeus hates busybodies," wrote Euripides. Think of how powerful it could be if just ten percent of the population took a "no humiliation" pledge, and rejected cruel or gossipy communications. Be part of that ten percent.

Lesson
NINE

Quantum Physics and the Mind

A growing wave of New Age books and documentaries use quantum theory to "prove" the idea that *thoughts are causative*. Many quantum physicists protest that crystal gazers have mangled the implications of these experiments, in which measurements of subatomic particles are affected by the presence or decisions of an observer.

The truth is: quantum physics *does* raise extraordinary questions about the nature of the mind.

More than eighty years of laboratory experiments demonstrate that atomic-scale particles appear in a given place only when a measurement is made. Astonishing as it sounds—and physicists themselves have debated the data

for generations—quantum theory holds that
*no measurement means no precise and localized
object*, on the atomic level.

Put differently, a subatomic particle literally occupies an infinite number of places (a
state called "superposition") until observation
manifests it in one place. In quantum mechan-
ics, a decision to look or not look actually determines what will be there. In this sense, an
observer's consciousness determines objective
reality in the subatomic field.

Some physicists would dispute that char-
acterization. Critics sometimes argue that certain particles are too small to measure; hence
any attempt at measurement inevitably affects
what is seen. But there exists a whole class of
"interaction-free measurement" quantum experiments that don't involve detectors at all.
Such experiments have repeatedly shown that
a subatomic object literally exists in more than
one place at once until a measurement determines its final resting spot.

How is this actually provable? In the par-
lance of quantum physics, an atomic-scale
particle is said to exist in a wave-state, which
means that the location of the particle in
space-time is known only probabilistically; it
has no properties in this state, just potentiali-
ties. When particles or waves – typically in the
form of a beam of photons or electrons – are

directed or aimed at a target system, such as a double-slit, scientists have found that their pattern or path will actually change, or "collapse," depending upon the presence or measurement choices of an observer. Hence, a wave pattern will shift into a particle pattern. Contrary to all reason, quantum theory holds that opposing outcomes simultaneously exist.

The situation gets even stranger when dealing with the thought experiment known as "Schrodinger's cat." The twentieth-century physicist Erwin Schrodinger was frustrated with the evident absurdity of quantum theory, which showed objects simultaneously appearing in more than one place at a time. Such an outlook, he felt, violated all commonly observed physical laws. In 1935, Schrodinger sought to highlight this predicament through a purposely absurdist thought experiment, which he intended to force quantum physicists to follow their data to its ultimate ends.

Schrodinger reasoned that quantum data dictates that a sentient being, such as a cat, can be simultaneously alive and dead. A variant of the "Schrodinger's cat" experiment could be put this way: Let's say a cat is placed into one of a pair of boxes. Along with the cat is what Schrodinger called a "diabolical device." The device, if exposed to an atom, releases a deadly poison. An observer then fires an atom at the boxes. The observer subsequently uses some form of measurement to check on which box the atom is in: the empty one, or the one with the cat and the poisoning device. When the observer goes to check, the wave function of the atom—i.e., the state in which it exists in both boxes—collapses into a particle function—i.e., the state in which it is localized to one box. Once the observer takes his measurement, convention says that the cat will be discovered to be dead or alive. But Schrodinger reasoned that quantum physics describes an outcome in which the cat is *both* dead and alive. This is because the atom, in its wave function, was, at one time, in either box, and either outcome is real.

To take it even further, a cohort of quantum physicists in the 1950s theorized that if an observer waited some significant length of time, say, eight hours, before checking on the dead-alive cat, he would discover one cat that was dead for eight hours and another that was alive for eight hours (and is now hungry). In this line of reasoning, conscious observation effectively manifested the localized atom, the dead cat, the living cat—and *also manifested the past*, i.e., created a history for both a dead cat and a living one. Both outcomes are true.

Absurd? Impossible? Yes to that, say quantum physicists—but decades of quantum experiments make this model—in which a creature can be dead/alive—into an impossible reality: an unbelievable yet entirely tenable, even necessary, state of nature. Only future experiments will determine the broader implications of sub-atomic phenomena in the mechanical world in which we live.

For now, however, decades of quantum data make it defensible to conclude that observation done on the subatomic scale: (1) shapes the nature of outcomes, (2) determines the presence or absence of a localized object, and (3) possibly devises multiple pasts and presents. This last point is sometimes called the "many-worlds interpretation," in the words of physicist Hugh Everett. This theory of "many worlds" raises the prospect of an infinite number of realities and states of being, each depending upon our choices. And here we encounter the frustrating but persistent thesis of positive thinking, which holds, in some greater or lesser measure, that our thoughts affect reality.

For our next and final lesson we will explore a dynamic philosopher whose ideas provide the closest New Thought analog to quantum theory.

Lesson
TEN

Neville Goddard, Explorer of the Infinite

In our previous lesson, I mentioned the theories of quantum physicist Hugh Everett. Everett theorized the existence of "multiple worlds" and outcomes based on the choices and perspective of the observer. His way of thought finds its closest metaphysical analog in the work of Neville Goddard (1905–1972), a mystical writer and lecturer who reasoned that our thoughts create an infinitude of realities and outcomes.

Neville (who went by his first name) taught that everything we see and experience is the product of what happens in our own individual dream of reality. Through a combination of emotional conviction and mental images, Neville said, each person imagines his own world into being—all people and events are rooted in us, as we are ultimately rooted in God. When a person awakens to his true self, Neville argued, he will, in fact, discover himself to be a slumbering branch of the Creator clothed in human form, and at the helm of infinite possibilities.

Neville's formula was simplicity itself: *First*, clarify you desire. *Second*, assume a state of physical immobility, a deeply relaxed state similar to what you experience just before drifting to sleep. *Third*, enact in your mind a small, satisfying drama that implies the wish fulfilled, such as someone congratulating you or your holding an award. Repeat this internal drama over and over, as long as it is vivid and emotionally charged.

"Take my challenge and put my words to the test," Neville told listeners in 1949. "If the law does not work, its knowledge will not comfort you. And if it is not true, you must discard it . . . I hope you will be bold enough to test me."

Most quantum physicists wouldn't be caught dead/alive as Schrodinger's cat reading an occult philosopher like Neville. Indeed, many physicists reject the notion of interpreting the larger implications of quantum data at all. "Shut up and calculate!" is the battle cry popularized by physicist N. David Mermin. The role of physics, critics insist, is to *measure things*—not, in Einstein's phrase, to lift "the veil that shrouds the Old One." Others adopt the opposite position: If physics isn't for explaining reality, then what *is* it for?

The latter principle may carry the day. A new generation of physicists and theorists, raised in the sixties and seventies—and open to questions of consciousness—is gaining prominence. Medical researcher Robert Lanza, M.D., of the Institute for Regenerative Medicine at Wake Forest University, uses quantum theory to argue that death itself is ultimately a mental phenomenon: we "die" only insofar as the mind perceives demise. Psychiatrist Jeffrey M. Schwartz of UCLA links quantum physics with his research into how thoughts alter brain biology, concluding that "directed, willed mental activity . . . generates a *physical* force."

Quantum physics brings us to a threshold of inquiry that may redefine what it means to be human in the twenty-first century, as much as evolution did in the Victorian age.

*   *   *

I began this course by saying that its aim was not to help you better organize your sock drawer, but to open a whole new window on your existence. I hope the experiment we've begun together leads to experiences that give you a radical new idea of the forces behind creativity.

We create not only by using physical acts and sensory data, but we participate in the world in a nonphysical manner. We influence aspects of our surrounding life and material existence through the agencies of awareness and thought. And that's no fantasy.

Quiz

1. The *one simple idea* behind this course is:
   - a) Laugh and the world laughs with you.
   - b) Thoughts are causative.
   - c) The Law of Attraction.
   - d) Dreams foretell events.

The correct answer is: b) Thoughts are causative.

2. The most important factor in any self-help program is:
   - a) Whether a friend does it with you.
   - b) The quality of the teacher.
   - c) The cognitive data that supports it.
   - d) Your hunger for self-change.

The correct answer is: d) Your hunger for self-change.

3. You should use affirmations just before going to sleep and just upon waking because:
   a) You remember them better.
   b) You won't disturb others.
   c) Your mind is at its most impressionable.
   d) You have the time.

The correct answer is: c) Your is mind is at its most impressionable.

4. Emile Coué discovered that his patients were helped by:
   a) Sunlight.
   b) A sense of hopeful expectancy.
   c) Chanting.
   d) Talk therapy.

The correct answer is: b) A sense of hopeful expectancy.

5. The process of autosuggestion is set in motion by what we think about:
   a) Ourselves.
   b) Our hobbies.
   c) Other people.
   d) Ourselves and other people.

The correct answer is: d) Ourselves and other people.

6. We live under:
   a) A single mental super-law.
   b) Many laws and forces.
   c) The Law of Thought Magnetism.
   d) Whims of fate.

The correct answer is: b) Many laws and forces.

7. A Master Mind Group consists of:
   a) Two or more people who provide
      mutual support.
   b) Experts.
   c) Medical professionals.
   d) Psychics.

The correct answer is: a) Two or more people who provide mutual support.

8. In quantum physics "superposition"
   means that a particle:
   a) Is in space.
   b) Cannot be detected.
   c) Occupies an infinite number of places.
   d) Binds with other particles.

The correct answer is: c) Occupies an infinite number of places.

9. The thought experiment called
    "Schrodinger's cat" demonstrates:
    a) Simultaneous states of reality.
    b) How to split the atom.
    c) The weight of sub-atomic particles.
    d) The nature of felines.

The correct answer is: a) Simultaneous states of reality.

10. The closest New Thought analog to
     quantum physics comes from:
     a) Emile Coué.
     b) Neville Goddard.
     c) Ted Kaptchuk.
     d) Erwin Schrodinger.

The correct answer is: b) Neville Goddard.

*   *   *

Thank you for taking this Master Class Course—and please check out the others in our Master Class series. I hope this short program provides you with lessons and ideas that you will experiment with and benefit from over the course of your life. You can always email me with questions at MasterClassWithMitch@ gmail.com.

About the Author

MITCH HOROWITZ is a writer and publisher with a lifelong interest in man's search for meaning. He is a PEN Award-winning historian and the author of *Occult America* and *One Simple Idea: How Positive Thinking Reshaped Modern Life.* Mitch has written on everything from the war on witches to the secret life of Ronald Reagan for *The New York Times, The Wall Street Journal, Salon,* and *Time.com. The Washington Post* says Mitch "treats esoteric ideas and movements with an even-handed intellectual studiousness that is too often lost in today's raised-voice discussions." Visit at www.MitchHorowitz.com and @MitchHorowitz.

Printed in the USA
CPSIA information can be obtained
at www.ICGtesting.com
JSHW012045140824
68134JS00034B/3272